Truth Is Stranger than Fiction

Presents

# NATURE SHOCKERS

Written by **Keltie Thomas**
Illustrated by **Greg Hall**

**Maple Tree Press Inc.**
51 Front Street East, Suite 200, Toronto, Ontario M5E 1B3
www.mapletreepress.com

Distributed in Canada by Raincoast Books
9050 Shaughnessy Street, Vancouver, British Columbia V6P 6E5

Distributed in the United States by Publishers Group West
1700 Fourth Street, Berkeley, California 94710

**Dedication**
For P-J with much love

**Cataloguing in Publication Data**
Thomas, Keltie
        Nature shockers / Keltie Thomas ; illustrations by Greg Hall

(Planet earth news)
Includes index.
ISBN 1-897066-29-5 (bound).—ISBN 1-897066-30-9 (pbk.)

    1. Nature—Miscellanea—Juvenile literature. 2. Natural
history—Miscellanea—Juvenile literature. 3. Curiosities and
wonders—Juvenile literature. I. Hall, Greg, 1963- II. Title. III. Series.

QH48.T46 2005          j508          C2005-901177-7

Design, art direction & illustration: Greg Hall

We acknowledge the financial support of the Canada Council for the Arts,
the Ontario Arts Council, the Government of Canada through the Book
Publishing Industry Development Program (BPIDP), and the Government of
Ontario through the Ontario Media Development Corporation's Book
Initiative for our publishing activities.

ONTARIO ARTS COUNCIL
CONSEIL DES ARTS DE L'ONTARIO

Printed in China

A     B     C     D     E     F

**Acknowledgments**
Special thanks to all the wonderful people
at Maple Tree Press, especially Sheba,
Anne, and Victoria, and to designer and
artist extraordinaire Greg Hall.
Many thanks also to all the experts and
scientists who generously took the time to
read through the text and contribute many
helpful suggestions: George Billingsley,
US Geological Survey; Francis R. Cook,
Editor, *Canadian Field-Naturalist*;
Rod Crawford, Curator of Arachnids,
Burke Museum, University of Washington,
Seattle; Brenda Jones and the curators
of the Vancouver Aquarium Marine
Science Centre; Jean-Marc Moncalvo,
Curator of Fungi, Department of Natural
History, Centre for Biodiversity and
Conservation Biology, Royal Ontario
Museum; Dr. Krista Nelson, The Animal
Clinic; Andre Ngo, Centre for Biodiversity
and Conservation Biology, Royal Ontario
Museum; David Phillips, Senior
Climatologist, Environment Canada;
Kathleen Ryan, University of Manitoba;
Dr. Ian Shelton, David Dunlap
Observatory; Alan T. Whittemore,
US National Arboretum.

# Contents

# EARTH:

There's no place in the universe that has such strange goings-on as Earth—the blue-and-green planet, third in line from the Sun. Where else can you find deep blue oceans awash with bubbles that sink boats, and sea monsters no one has ever seen alive? Where else can you find trees that lock bikes in their trunks? Or rocks that walk? Or cats born bald? Or hair that grows on wood? Or polar bears that turn green?

And if you think that makes Earth sound kind of alien, you're absolutely right. So far Earth is the only known place in the universe where life exists. The sun-splashed orb is not too hot and not too cold. Its temperature is just right for life to rise up and rule. And that's exactly what makes Earth so extraordinary. Read on for the inside scoop on how life on Earth is stranger than fiction.

# There's No Place Like It

## Spot the
## Hoax Busters

Keep your wits about you as you travel around Earth. Earthlings have been known to exaggerate to tell a good story, and some love to pull a trick, or hoax, that fools fellow Earthlings. Use the Hoax Busters activities throughout this book to develop your sense of phony baloney. Consider each scene under the magnifying glass by asking yourself questions such as: Could the phenomenon be caused by other means or forces? If so, what ones? Check your answers on page 63 and keep score to see how you rate as a Hoax Buster.

# Earth Has a Twin Sister!

**V**enus is Earth's long, lost twin! Separated at birth, the two planets are almost the same size and mass, and have the same gravity—the force that holds things to their surfaces.

That was the sensational story that traveled around the world in 1761, when a Russian scientist discovered that Venus was covered by a thick blanket of white swirling clouds. Naturally, scientists assumed that the clouds were made of water—just like those on Earth. And since Venus is closer to the

The twins' first orbit.

Sun, it must be hotter, they reasoned. With that, visions of Venus as a tropical world awash in boiling oceans and thick swamps crawling with reptiles danced in their heads.

These wild ideas persisted for 200 years. In 1962, space technology allowed scientists to send an unmanned space probe to Venus for a closer look. *Mariner 2* beamed back data that revealed that the surface of Venus was 427°C (800°F)—hot enough to fry an egg on rocks! What's more, the planet's veil of clouds turned out to be made of a substance similar to battery acid! So much for being Earth's twin.

Even the imaginations of cavemen could have been lit by Venus. Apart from the Sun and Moon, it's the brightest natural object in the sky.

# CHAPTER 1

# Deep Creeps

Earth's oceans are deep, dark, and mysterious. Vast pools of water plunge down, down, down, into pitch-black valleys, mountains, and trenches far below the Sun's long reach.

The oceans account for nearly three-quarters of the planet, yet they remain largely unexplored. Earthlings have better maps of the dark side of the Moon and Mars than the ocean floor!

The deep blue sea is a truly alien world where you may meet fish who cut through water and rogue waves that freak out. Dive into the *Planet Earth News* exclusive on this underwater world, where you just never know what may lurk below.

Plunge into a breathtaking adventure.

# Something's Fishy

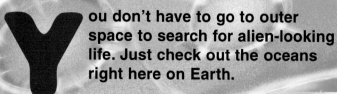

**Y**ou don't have to go to outer space to search for alien-looking life. Just check out the oceans right here on Earth.

## UFO Hovers
### in the Swim

**N**ot many creatures look as alien as jellyfish. Catch sight of one and you might think a flying saucer with snakelike tentacles is invading the deep! Nevertheless, these soft-bodied swimmers have been living on Earth for more than 650 million years—before dinosaurs ever set foot on the planet.

Jellies have no brain, no heart, no bones, and no eyes. But that's no problem for them. An inner network of nerves helps jellies sense food and danger. Tentacles studded with stingers allow the fish to latch onto prey and defend themselves. What's more, the stingers of some jellies are lethal weapons!

## FISH SAWS
## through Water

**H**i-ho! Hi-ho! It's off to saw we go. The sawfish cruises through the Atlantic, Indian, and Pacific oceans with a long bladelike snout that has pointy teeth along both sides. It's a handy tool for warding off predators like a sword, and sensing movements of prey in the distance. What's more, it can detect the heartbeat of prey buried in sand then dig them up. Despite this fearsome blade, experts say sawfish are gentle creatures that like to hang out in mud on the sea floor. Can you dig it, er, saw it?

## There's a Blob
## in My Soup!

**B**illions of years ago a strange blob arose. It was unlike anything the galaxy had ever seen. It came to be in the ocean on Earth—the murky chemical soup that covered the planet. At first it was only the tiniest little mite, but the blob eventually became the biggest force on the planet. It was the first form of life, and over millions of years plants, fish, reptiles, jaguars, monkeys, human beings, and all Earth's creatures followed in its wake.

# Godzilla Goes Up in Smoke

Hot vents in the ocean floor are smokin'. No joke! In fact, they're called "black smokers." The hot black smoke, containing chemicals, shoots up into the cool seawater and forms solid deposits that grow into chimneylike columns. The chimneys grow about 2.5 cm (1 in.) a day. One of the largest ever found was as tall as a 13-story building. Scientists called it Godzilla and eventually it went up in smoke, collapsing under its own weight or the force of an earthquake. But Godzilla has been inching its way back up. Maybe there's just no way to keep a good monster down!

# Lipstick Gives Life New Look

Beyond the reach of sunlight, the bottom of the sea is a cold, watery world darker than the darkest night. Convinced that life could not survive there, scientists were floored when tubeworms—creatures that look like giant tubes of lipstick—were discovered in 1977. Tubeworms live in the darkness near hot vents in the sea floor, surviving on a chemical from the vents that's deadly to most living things. And that's how "lipstick" gave life a whole new look!

# Unidentified Blob Lands on Beach?

Oh, no, it's *The Blob*! Movie-goers cringed in their seats, watching giant blobs of alien goo try to take over Earth in this 1950s science-fiction flick. Luckily, Earthlings have yet to come across any such things beyond the world of fiction. But every few years, a massive unidentified blob washes ashore and people think it's a sea monster. In 2003, a 13-ton blob of gray flesh washed up in Chile. Scientists investigated and discovered it was the remains of a whale. When whales die, their bones and muscles fall away, leaving a floating blob of skin. In fact, recent tests show that beached blobs dating back to 1896 are all whales.

# Dragonfish Burns Prey

It doesn't breathe fire, but the dragonfish, found at great depths in oceans around the world, burns like a nightlight in the pitch-black deep. To lure prey, a "fishing rod," or barbel, on its chin lights up, as well as organs along each side of its body. No longer than a human hand, the dragonfish is one of the ocean's most ferocious predators. It will eat anything in sight— including prey much larger than itself!

# The Mighty Sea

Earth's oceans are always in motion. And sometimes wind, tides, and currents can stir up one serious commotion.

# Wave Freaks Out

Some waves freak out big-time. No kidding! They turn into freak, or rogue, waves that have the size and power to wipe out a large ship in a single go. Sailors have been telling tales of freak waves half as wide as a football field and as tall as an office tower for hundreds of years. They say the monster water-walls rise straight up out of nowhere, followed by a deep trough like a hole in the sea. But, until recently, many scientists thought rogue waves were just a myth. Now they've discovered that freak waves are the culprit in many ship sinkings, and are likely to occur where a swell crashes into a swirling current called an eddy.

# Bubbles Sink Boat

Poof! A ship disappears without a trace in the North Sea or the Bermuda Triangle. Pop goes the familiar story as no remains turn up, nor any explanation. But now, some scientists think they may have solved the mystery behind these strange disappearances. They say the ocean floor has pockets of solid methane in the North Sea and the Bermuda Triangle. When an earthquake or rising temperatures disturb these pockets, the scientists think the solid methane turns into bubbles of gas. The bubbles rising to the surface mix with the ocean water, making the water less dense. If the water becomes less dense than a ship floating on top of it, the ship can sink. Bloop!

## Sneakers Track Ocean Currents

Kicks overboard! In 1990, a huge storm tossed 80,000 brand-new sneakers from a cargo ship into the Pacific Ocean near Korea. The floating shoes were swept up by currents that flow through the ocean like enormous rivers. The currents took them on a wild ride that scattered them all over the world. In 1991, waves of the sneakers began running ashore in Oregon. Once ocean researcher Curtis Ebbesmeyer heard about the soggy kicks, he thought the sneakers could help reveal how currents move around the ocean. He tracked the floating sneakers to beaches in western Canada, northern California, Washington, Hawaii, the Philippines, and Japan. His work has helped reveal how ocean currents flow and tell where "goods overboard" will eventually turn up.

## EXPOSED!

Long ago, whales could hop out of the ocean and walk on land. Scientists have found ancient whale fossils with sheeplike anklebones. Now that's something to "Baa" home about!

## TIDE MAKES RIVER RUN BACKWARDS

Every day, all the oceans on Earth flow toward shore and away from shore. It's a regular cycle we call the tides. An incoming tide is a flood, or high tide. An outgoing tide is an ebb, or low tide. Residents around the St. John River in New Brunswick, Canada, say high tide makes the river run backwards. They say the river, which usually flows toward the Bay of Fundy, flows away from the bay at high tide.

**Do you think this is...**

A) a fake claim to fame?
B) an optical illusion?
C) a quirk of nature?
D) a neat 'n' tidy phenomenon?

Answer on page 63.

## Something's Eating the Titanic

Something is munching its way through the wreck of the *Titanic*, the cruise ship that smashed into an iceberg in 1912 and sank with 1,500 people on board. Sound fishy? The voracious creature is no plant or animal, or even a monster. Scientists say it's a rusticle: a group of tiny bacteria that form rusty icicles as they cling to the wreck and gobble up its iron. The rusticles are weakening the wreck faster than the sea's forces of water and pressure. So even though the *Titanic* rests on the bottom of the deep blue sea, it's still falling to pieces. Go figure!

# M-m-monster Dead Ahead!

**O**h, there are no monsters like sea monsters, like no monsters we know. Get the scoop!

## Sea Monsters Get Real

**S**plash, lash—and dash! It's the tale of many a sea monster that sailors have been telling for hundreds of years. A sea serpent with a head as big as a barrel and tentacles for arms rises up from the deep. Splash! It wraps its arms around a ship— lash!— then pulls it under and vanishes without a trace. Dash! Now, scientists think sea monsters may be real creatures—giant squid that live down deep. Though they've never seen a live one, they've found dead giant squid washed ashore that look the part. The squid have eight octopus-like arms coming out of their heads, two long tentacles for grasping prey, and a razor-sharp beak. And they're massive—as long as one and a half school buses parked end to end.

# PLANET EARTH'S MOST WANTED?

Many people claim to have spotted these lake monsters. But not one monster has ever been caught to prove its existence. Check out this gallery of legendary monsters still at large.

**NESSIE**

Lair: Loch Ness, Scotland
Spotted: Surfacing in a photograph

**LAKE VAN MONSTER**

Lair: Lake Van, Turkey
Spotted: On the move with head and humps above water

**OGOPOGO**

Lair: Lake Okanagan, Canada
Spotted: Making waves with a horselike head and body of a snake

**CHAMP**

Lair: Lake Champlain, U.S.
Spotted: Raising a slender neck out of the water

**SELMA**

Lair: Lake Seljordsvatnet, Norway
Spotted: Slithering into the water and attacking a small boat

**NAHUELITO**

Lair: Nahuel Huapi Lake, Argentina
Spotted: Sending up a spray of water as its snakelike head appears

presents **Tales That Got Us**

# Monster Not Legend but Fact

Nessie always seems to make a splash. The legendary monster that lurks in Scotland's lake Loch Ness has been making headline news around the world for years. "Monster of Loch Ness Is Not Legend But a Fact," claimed the front page of London's *Daily Mail* in 1933.

In 1934, Nessie made a headline splash again. Colonel Robert Wilson, a highly respected surgeon, snapped a photo that showed the long neck of a sea serpent rising out of Loch Ness. Experts examined the shot and found no evidence of tampering. So in lieu of any living proof, the photo became the next-best

**Nessie's secret identity.**

evidence of Nessie's existence. But in 1994, Christian Spurling revealed the photo was a fake. He said the monster in the shot was nothing but a plastic sea-serpent head stuck to a toy submarine!

Over the years, several scientists have searched the lake with sonar—sound waves that bounce off objects. And though they've found large, unexplained objects, none have turned up any solid proof of Nessie's existence. Nevertheless, many people believe it's a mystery that would be solved "if only the real Loch Ness monster would please stand up!"

**Loch Ness lies on shifty ground. An average of three earthquakes rock the lake every hundred years.**

# CHAPTER 2

# It's a Jungle Out There

The plants on Earth are green, mean survival machines. They make their own food from sunlight, and grow in every environment on the planet from the salty seas to bone-dry deserts. Life on Earth just wouldn't be the same without the green stuff.

Long ago, primitive plants pumped up the Earth's atmosphere with oxygen, which nearly all living creatures need to breathe. To this day, plants remain one of the largest sources of oxygen on Earth. So take a deep breath and let this *Planet Earth News* exclusive root you to the spot with the remarkable lives of plants and trees.

Enter at your own risk....

# Vicious Vines

**P**lants will stop at nothing to survive. Check out how some tackle the roots of the problem by laying traps for buggy meals, spreading seeds via "the animal express," and making a big stink.

## Flower Smells Like
# ROTTING FLESH

**I**t's big, it's rare, and boy does it stink! The endangered Rafflesia flower, which grows on the rain forest floor in Sumatra and Borneo, is the largest flower in the world. In full bloom, it can stretch as much as 0.9 m (3 ft.) wide and weigh up to 11 kg (25 lbs.). And it makes a big stink that smells like a dead fish. P-U! In fact, locals call it the "stinking corpse lily." The foul odor attracts flies and beetles that like to eat rotting flesh. As they hang out on the flower, they pick up pollen then carry it to other flowers, helping the Rafflesia reproduce.

# Hun
## Plant

**T**rapped, zapped, and devoured for dinner. That's how hapless bugs will end up when they land on the open leaves of a Venus flytrap. This lip-smacking, er, leaf-trapping plant found in swamps of North and South Carolina is a genuine carnivore, or meat-eater. The Venus flytrap lures insects with sweet-smelling nectar, and its spike-tipped leaves are like a spring-loaded trap. Once a bug touches two trigger-hairs on the leaves, they

## Orchid Grows
## Undercover as BEE

**T**he mirror orchid mimics a female bee to a T. The Mediterranean flower's shimmering blue lip, or "mirror," has a yellow border, hairy red fringe, and side lobes that look like insect wings. And it doesn't rely on looks alone. The orchid also gives off a special

# gry Snaps

snap shut around the bug in a deadly embrace. If the unlucky bug is large enough—fly-size or bigger—it cannot escape through the "jailhouse bars" of the leaves' spikes. The leaves then seal shut completely, crushing the bug and drowning it in digestive fluids. A few days later, the leaves open, releasing the bug's empty shell and setting up for the next meal to drop in.

chemical that smells just like a female bee looking to mate. Fooled, male bees land on the flower only to be rapped on the head by a stalk of pollen. Then the bees buzz off to the next orchid, unwittingly spreading the pollen to help the flower reproduce. Mission accomplished!

## Thorny Hitchhikers Dead Ahead

When it comes to spreading seeds, the South African devil's claw is all thumbs-up. Its seed pod looks like a tiny octopus with thorn-tipped arms. The pod hitches a ride with any rhino or elephant that strolls along by hooking a thorn into the animal's foot. Then the creature treads on the pod with each step. Finally, the pod bursts, dispersing seeds in a new spot. It's a pain in the foot!

## UFOS MAKE CROP CIRCLES

Strange circles began appearing in farmers' fields in England in the 1970s. Whatever, or whoever, made the circles did it under cover of the night. So no one caught a glimpse of the action. Later, the mysterious circles began showing up in other parts of the world, too. Rumor had it that they were made by alien spaceships landing.

**Were the circles made by...**

A) hoaxers with too much time on their hands?
B) round UFOs landing on the fields?
C) weird weather?
D) extraterrestrials leaving Earthlings a sign?
E) advertisers trying to catch people's attention?

Answer on page 63.

## Cucumber Takes Off Like Rocket

The Mediterranean squirting cucumber doesn't hang around waiting for the "animal express" to roll through and spread its seeds. It does the job on its own steam. As its seeds ripen, the cucumber fills up with slimy juice. This liquid builds up lots of pressure inside the cucumber. When the pressure becomes too great to bear, the cucumber explodes off its stalk like a rocket. The squirting fruit falls to the ground as its seeds shoot through the air with a trail of slime streaming out behind them. Three, two, one…blastoff!

# Branching Out

Trees stand rooted to the spot. But make no mistake, when it comes to survival, they definitely get around the seedy heart of the jungle. Check out some of the tricks they have up their sleeves, er, leaves.

## Tree Has a Blast Monkeying Around

Bang! A sharp pistollike sound rings through the jungle when the sandbox tree launches its seeds. Also known as the "dynamite tree" and "monkey pistol," the fruit of this Central and South American tree looks like a wooden tangerine, and holds the seeds. Once the fruit ripens, it explodes with a loud bang, bursting into tangerinelike segments and firing the seeds as far as 12 m (40 ft.). The sound is enough to make people run for cover. Talk about monkeying around with a blast! But the seeds and sap of the tree are no laughing matter. They're extremely poisonous—touch them and red welts may break out on your skin. What's more, if animals eat them they may vomit or drop dead. You might say the monkey pistol fires a lethal bullet.

## Pirate Tree Sails the Sea

Maybe the seed of the coconut palm tree should be called "Captain Nutcase." Not only is it encased inside a coconut the size of a human head, but it resembles the face of a monkey (three pores on the shell look like eyes and a mouth), and it can sail the sea like a pirate. Coconut palm trees grow on many tropical shores around the world, sending out seeds as their coconuts fall to the ground. Kerplunk! Splash! Some coconuts roll out to sea then float for thousands of kilometres till they wash ashore and put down roots to plunder the land's nutrient riches. Palm loco to go-go!

# ATTACK of Killer Plants?

A hundred years ago, people-eating trees and killer plants that grew in far-flung places were the stuff of many a legend. And in 1951, John Wyndham wrote *The Day of the Triffids*—a science-fiction story in which giant carnivorous, or meat-eating, plants attack people. The Triffids' goal was to eliminate the human race and take over Earth. But what makes the story particularly creepy is that the Triffids have some characteristics of real carnivorous plants. Luckily, there's not much chance that huge plants capable of consuming people could exist. That's because it would take a lot of energy to digest an organism as big as a human being. In fact, when a Venus flytrap tries to digest a meal bigger than it can handle, its leaf that trapped the meal turns black and dies. The end!

# Tree LOCKS BIKE in Trunk

Just how did this Douglas fir tree in Vashon Island, Washington, trap a bike inside its trunk? Nobody knows. But one thing's certain: it's not about to let the bike go anytime soon. The tree holds the bike 2 m (7 ft.) above the ground and its bark has wound around the bike frame, embedding the bike in the trunk. Chances are the bike was left in the fork of the tree about 40 years ago. Since this strange story hit the news, a few people have come forward, claiming to own the bike. One woman says the bike broke down when she was 13 years old. So she put it on top of a "Christmas tree." Meanwhile, a man says that he hunted frogs around the tree as a kid, and forgot his bike there. And so the mystery of the bike goes round and round….

# The Forest STRANGLER Strikes Again

The strangler fig takes no prisoners. Once this tropical tree springs to life, it goes to work like a boa constrictor. The strangler fig surrounds the trunk of an unsuspecting tree, slowly squeezing the life right out of it. Bats and birds do some of its dirty work, too. They eat the strangler's sweet-tasting figs, which hold seeds. Then they poop on the fly, dumping the seeds onto the branches of other trees. The seeds then send down snakelike roots around the victim's trunk, eventually encasing the tree all the way to the ground. Without light and room to grow, the tree rots, leaving the strangler fig in its place. How's that for a real snake in the grass, er, woods!

# SPAGHETTI GROWS
## on Trees

O n April 1, 1957, the British Broadcasting Corporation (BBC) gave viewers a little something to use their noodles on. News anchor Richard Dimbleby reported that an uncommonly mild winter had left Switzerland with a huge spaghetti crop. And the kicker? The newscast showed images of a Swiss family picking spaghetti off trees. "For those who love this dish, there's nothing like real, home-grown spaghetti," Dimbleby signed off.

Immediately, hundreds of viewers began calling in.

A "saucy" tree.

Brrring! Brrring! "Does spaghetti really grow on trees?" they asked. "How do I grow my own spaghetti tree?"

"Place a sprig of spaghetti in a tin of tomato sauce and hope for the best," the BBC replied. But eventually they fessed up: the whole report was an April Fools' joke. Ha-ha!

So why did the story foil, er, boil so many a British noodle? Back then, not much pasta was eaten in Britain and how it was made was a bit of a mystery. What's more, like most people around the world, the Brits trusted TV news to report the facts and nothing but.

What may have bugged viewers most was the BBC's attention to faking detail. It claimed the high spaghetti yield was due to the disappearance of a "spaghetti weevil" pest.

# CHAPTER 3

# Grime Time

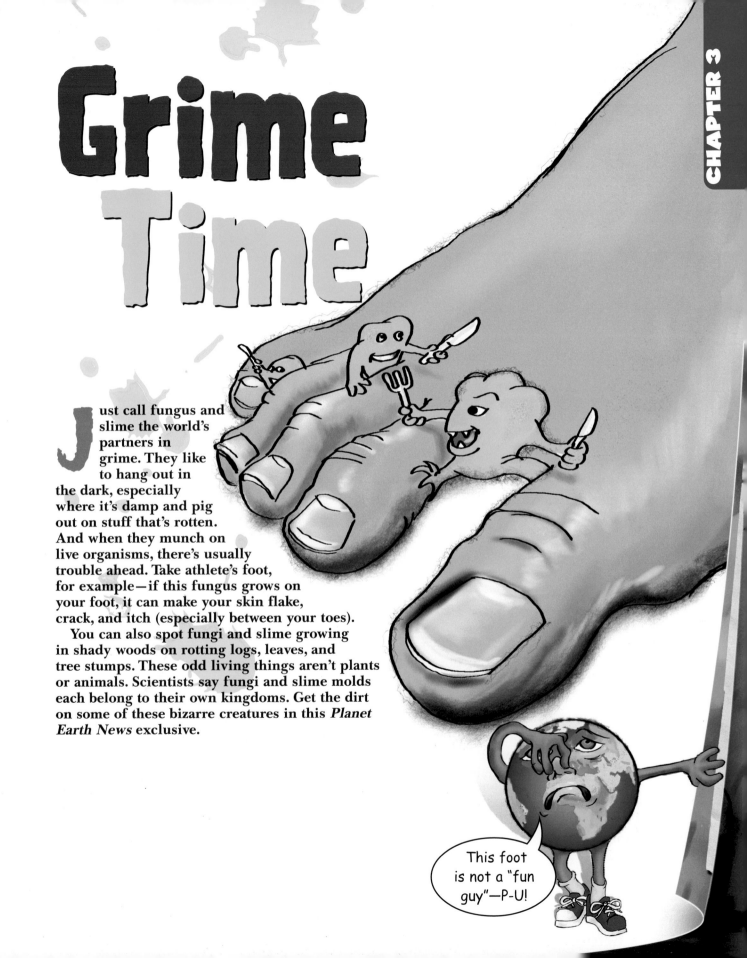

**J**ust call fungus and slime the world's partners in grime. They like to hang out in the dark, especially where it's damp and pig out on stuff that's rotten. And when they munch on live organisms, there's usually trouble ahead. Take athlete's foot, for example—if this fungus grows on your foot, it can make your skin flake, crack, and itch (especially between your toes).

You can also spot fungi and slime growing in shady woods on rotting logs, leaves, and tree stumps. These odd living things aren't plants or animals. Scientists say fungi and slime molds each belong to their own kingdoms. Get the dirt on some of these bizarre creatures in this *Planet Earth News* exclusive.

This foot is not a "fun guy"—P-U!

# Fungus Among Us

**P**ssst. Don't look now but there's a fungus among us. In fact, there's more than one. We likely share Earth with more than a million different types of fungi. Check out a massive fungus that can grow right under your nose without you ever knowing!

## ICEMAN Earns Medical Doctorate

**Ö**tzi the Iceman is a 5,300-year-old mummy. He was discovered in 1991, carrying two walnut-sized lumps of birch fungus strung on leather thongs that may have tied around his wrist or belt. Scientists think he may have used the fungus as strong medicine like antibiotics.

## Humongous Fungus
### Busts the Scale

**S**omething's growing in the woods of Michigan. It's lurking under the ground, gobbling up rotting wood, and feasting on live tree roots. It's a humongous fungus that covers 15 hectares (37 acres) and weighs almost as much as a blue whale. What's more, it's been hunkered down there for at least 1,500 years with no one the wiser.

It's "one of the oldest and largest organisms on Earth," say the scientists who found it in 1992. The fact that something so large could live among us unnoticed for so long blew people's minds. Just how did the fungus become so humongous? Fungus grows by sending out shoestringlike tendrils under the ground, enabling the fungus to survive and thrive in areas poor in nutrients. Since then scientists have found bigger fungi lurking in our midst.

# SHOTGUN FUNGUS
## Hits Bull's-Eye

Pow! The fungus jumped over the cow—and how. Shaped like a miniature lightbulb on a stalk, the shotgun fungus stands in its ground-level cow dung home. All of a sudden, its bulb explodes, firing a clump of spores, or seeds—foomp! The clump lands on grass in front of the cow. The cow goes on grazing without missing a beat and gobbles up the spores along with the grass. Mission accomplished! The shotgun fungus has successfully "planted" its spores in a cow's body. Now the tough, indigestible spores can travel through the cow's guts and come out the other end in bovine dung—the perfect environment for growing more shotgun fungus. Bull's-eye!

## EXPOSED!

The giant puffball mushroom explodes in a huff, er, puff. It cracks open so its spores, or tiny seeds, can hitch a ride on the wind.

## Hoax Busters

# FAIRY RING
## APPEARS OVERNIGHT

Early one morning, two hikers discovered a fairy ring—a group of mushrooms growing in a circle. Legend has it that mushroom rings are magically made by fairies dancing in the middle of the night.

**Do you think it was...**

A) a bogus specimen that's been faked?
B) a phenomenon of nature?
C) a ring made by fairies dancing in a circle?
D) an April Fools' joke planted by local yokels?

Answer on page 63.

# KILLER FUNGUS
## Snags Worm

Dead meat. That's what a roundworm is if *Dactylella* fungus catches it. Growing as a cluster of fingerlike threads, or hyphae, *Dactylella* set "worm traps" by forming lassoes. Once a worm sticks its head or tail in a lasso, there's no escape. The lasso tightens like a noose and strangles the worm to death. Sound cruel? Hey, when you're a fungus, you can't make your own food like plants do, or move to find food like animals. So you've got to snag some grub any which way you can!

# Oozing Along Now

**A**re you ready to be totally slimed? Take cover and get a close-up look at some slime molds and other creatures that deal in oodles of ooze.

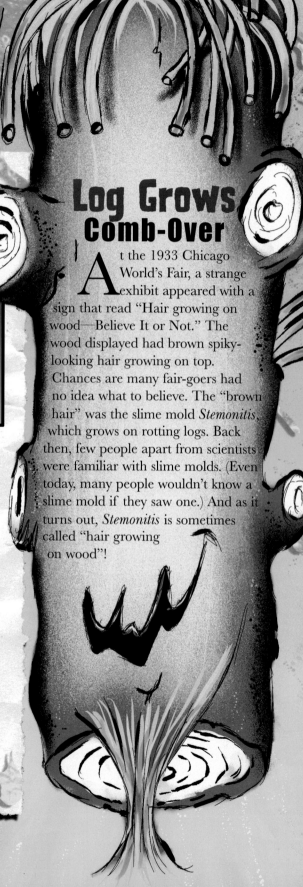

## Log Grows
### Comb-Over

**A**t the 1933 Chicago World's Fair, a strange exhibit appeared with a sign that read "Hair growing on wood—Believe It or Not." The wood displayed had brown spiky-looking hair growing on top. Chances are many fair-goers had no idea what to believe. The "brown hair" was the slime mold *Stemonitis*, which grows on rotting logs. Back then, few people apart from scientists were familiar with slime molds. (Even today, many people wouldn't know a slime mold if they saw one.) And as it turns out, *Stemonitis* is sometimes called "hair growing on wood"!

## Smart Slime
### Solves Maze

**I**n the year 2000, a blob of yellow slime stunned scientists when it found the shortest path through a maze. Scientists divided the slime blob into pieces and stuck each piece at different points in the maze. Then they put out food at the maze's entrance and exit. And get this: all the little pieces of slime joined back together to form a wormlike tube that stretched itself out along the shortest path between the maze's entrance and exit. The scientists said that this showed the slime mold has intelligence. Other scientists disagreed. They said the blob was just going about its everyday business, sensing the location of food, then changing shape to move in on it for a tasty meal. Either way, you might say the slime made a smart move to survive. What do you think?

Str**a**ng**e**
BUT
Tr**u**e

# EXPOSED!

In Mexico, "scrambled egg" slime mold is a yummy treat. It's collected when it comes out at night, scrambled like eggs, and eaten!

## Foot Turns Into Surfboard

Snails glide on a slimy "muscular foot." When the tide rolls out, the plough snail of South Africa rides its foot like a surfboard. The snail surfs the waves along the beach to hunt down a meal.

# SLIMY
# Escape Artist
# Ties Itself into Knot

You do "knot" want to mess with the hagfish, a.k.a slime eel. When predators or any other hapless creatures disturb it, the hagfish slimes them—and itself! The provoked creature secretes globs of gooey slime from 75 to 100 glands along the sides of its body. The thick goop surrounds the hagfish almost instantly, and thin threads that run through it make the slime extremely sticky and strong. The sticky glop can clog fish gills so fish can't breathe. But you won't find the hagfish suffocating in its own slime. It has a cool trick up its "sheath" to escape the goop's sticky clutches. The hagfish ties itself into a knot then slips the knot along the length of its body to wipe away the slime. "Knot" bad for a fish!

# Alien Slime Takes Over Town

**P**anic broke out in Garland, Texas, in the summer of 1973, when large numbers of pulsating yellow slime blobs suddenly began appearing out of nowhere. The quivering blobs popped up in people's yards, crept along lawns, and climbed telephone poles. What's more, the strange things grew and spread themselves around.

People freaked! They thought the platter-sized blobs were mutant creatures sent to Earth by alien invaders. They called in firefighters to hose one

**Texans fear "blobbings."**

down off a telephone pole. But the blob just grew and slithered further up the pole. News reporters flocked to the scene to cover the story of "the blob that could not be stopped."

An unidentifed "Growing Object" terrorized Mrs. Marie Harris's backyard for three weeks, reported *Newsweek* on June 11, 1973. In fact, the fear of "blob sightings" didn't die down until a scientist identified the blobs as *Fuligo septica*, a harmless slime mold commonly found in North America.

Further scientific investigation revealed that an unusual amount of rain had drenched the area that spring, creating favorable conditions for the slime mold to take hold. And take hold it did—especially in people's imaginations.

Every now and then, police get a call from someone who has found a bizarre-looking slime mold and thinks aliens have landed.

Bizarre

# CHAPTER 4

# Where the Wild Things Are

E arth is a total zoo. A myriad of different species of animals wander the planet. Since animals can't make their own food like plants do, they're usually on the move in search of a meal. Or else they're trying to avoid the jaws of another hungry animal!

Is it any wonder Earth's animals have developed remarkable bodies, survival moves, and senses that make them extremely hard to pin down? Check out this *Planet Earth News* exclusive to discover some extraordinary creatures whose behavior throws the world for a loop.

Run wild!

# Survival Moves

## Check out some of the odd moves Earth's creatures make in the daily game of survival.

# Amazing
## Lizard Feat

No, your eyes are not playing tricks on you. The basilisk lizard of Central and South America really runs on water! When the lizard senses danger, it stands up on its two hind legs, holds out its tail for balance, and skedaddles!

The lizard speeds away so fast that the large soles of its partly webbed feet don't sink into the water. But it can only keep its feet above water for a short spurt. As soon as the basilisk slows down, it falls into the drink. Splash!

# Bird Loops

The everyday maneuvers of a hummingbird are stiff competition for stunt pilots—let alone other birds. The tiny winged marvel of North and South America can fly sideways, backwards, and upside down. And its aerial acrobatics don't stop there. It can also somersault backwards and loop the loop—fly up, down, and

## Crab has
## Wicked Spitball

The sand bubbler crab of Australia and Malaysia is Earth's ace spitballer. When the daily tide goes out, the tiny crab covers the beach with small spitballs. No joke! The bug-eyed crab pokes its two eyes on long stalks out of its burrow and looks around, making sure the coast is clear of predators. Then it crawls out to feed on the nutrient-rich ooze that covers sand. Using its claws, it scrapes the sand and scoops it into its mouth, sifting out tiny bits of food. The crab then spits out the sand in the shape of a ball and crawls forward for another sandy bite. Soon, tiny balls of sand trail out from its burrow in a star pattern. How's that for a gritty pitcher who never lets up?

# the Loop!

around in a perfect circle. The little flying ace routinely tops stunt pilots by hovering on the spot in midair like a helicopter. But none of its moves are for show. The hummingbird hovers, swoops, and loops to get into position to drink the energy-rich nectar of flowers with its long bill. After all, flying requires lots of fuel!

## FISH WALKS TO NEW DIGS

When a local lake dried up, residents said a catfish threw in the towel—and walked out. The fish walked on the tips of its fins across land to another lake! What do you think?

Is this...

A) a likely story?
B) an optical illusion?
C) a true story of a walking fish?
D) a natural survival mechanism?

Answer on page 63.

## Froggy Wrestlers
# Rumble in the Jungle

The strawberry poison dart frog of Central and South America is no heavyweight. The brightly colored frog, whose skin secretes deadly poisons to protect it from hungry predators, is only about half the size of your thumb. But it's a world-class wrestler all the same. The male frog stakes out territory in its rain-forest habitat. And if another male tries to move in, he challenges the intruder to a wrestling match. The tiny frog chirps loudly and grabs his opponent around the middle. The frogs lock arms around each other and push strongly with their hind legs, trying to topple each other over. Once one frog falls, the other jumps on him and holds him down for a little while. Talk about being down for the count!

## EXPOSED!

An owl doesn't need eyes in the back of its head to spot prey. It can turn its head right around to look behind its back!

# What an Animal!

**P**ssst. Did you hear about the polar bears who turned green, the orangutan who picked locks, and the squirrels who stole golf balls? Sometimes Earth's animals do the strangest things. Check 'em out!

## Polar Bears Turn Green

**G**reen bears aren't glam. That was the story at the Singapore Zoo in 2004 when two polar bears—Sheba and her 13-year-old son Inuka—turned green. The fur coats of polar bears are made of clear, hollow hairs. Usually, the hairs look white, because they reflect light. In polar bears' Arctic habitat, this gives them the perfect camouflage among the snow and ice. Had someone spray-painted the bears to conceal them better in their tropical zoo home? No, said zoo officials. Tiny green plants called algae were the culprits. Singapore's warm and humid climate allowed the algae to settle inside the hollow hairs of the bears.

## Squirrelly Bandits Nab Golf Balls

**T**he red squirrels at the Riverside Golf Course in Edmonton, Canada, are notorious for having a ball. The little bandits stake out the tenth and eighteenth holes on the green then dash off with players' golf balls. The balls are stashed in the tops of tall trees. In fact, one tree had 250 balls tucked among its branches! Some scientists think the spunky squirrels steal golf balls because the balls look like mushrooms. But whatever the case may be, the balls are toast once these sharp-toothed critters chew them to bits. Talk about squirrelly!

## Hippo Sees Red

Do hippos sweat blood? That's what people once thought, because the burly beasts secrete a reddish-brown slime on their skin. However, recent research reveals that the gunk protects hippopotamuses from the Sun's rays like sunscreen does for us.

# Fu Manchu
## Escapes from Zoo

Locks just couldn't keep Fu Manchu behind bars. The orangutan who lived at the Omaha Zoo in 1968 broke out of his enclosure three times before zoo keepers caught on to his escape trick. The head zookeeper decided to keep watch and caught Fu Manchu in the act. He saw the big ape climb down into a dry moat and pull back a heavy door with brute strength. Then Fu Manchu took a wire out of his mouth and picked the lock. The American Association of Locksmiths was so impressed that Fu Manchu was made an honorary member!

## EXPOSED!

Bang on the glass walls of the chimpanzee enclosure at Chicago's Lincoln Park Zoo and you just may get tit for tat. A hidden button allows the chimps to shoot puffs of air at rowdy visitors!

# What on Earth...?

There's no way on Earth a creature could have the stripes of a zebra, the long tongue of an anteater, and the ears of a donkey. Or is there? Meet a couple of animals that people once thought were too bizarre to be real.

## "Donkey" Pins the Tale on Earthling

The okapi kicked up quite a ruckus when it was discovered by the world at large in 1901. Back then, the odd-looking animal with the stripes of a zebra, tongue of an anteater, and ears of a donkey was known only to locals who lived in the heart of the African jungle. But experts didn't believe such a thing could exist, because no wild donkeys lived in the area. It wasn't until they studied an okapi skin that locals' reports were found to be bang-on. A new animal had been found and Earthlings were thrilled. And get this: even though the okapi looks like a donkey and a zebra, it's actually a cousin of the giraffe. Could any animal be harder to pin down?

## Dragons

Mayday! Mayday! Legend has it that, in 1912, a pilot crash-landed on Komodo Island, Indonesia. The pilot lived to tell a tale of huge, fierce dragons that circled the wreckage of his plane searching for a meal. And it wasn't the first time dragons were spotted in the area. Locals told tales of "land crocodiles" that could take down water buffalo. The tales captured the interest of a Dutch lieutenant who went to

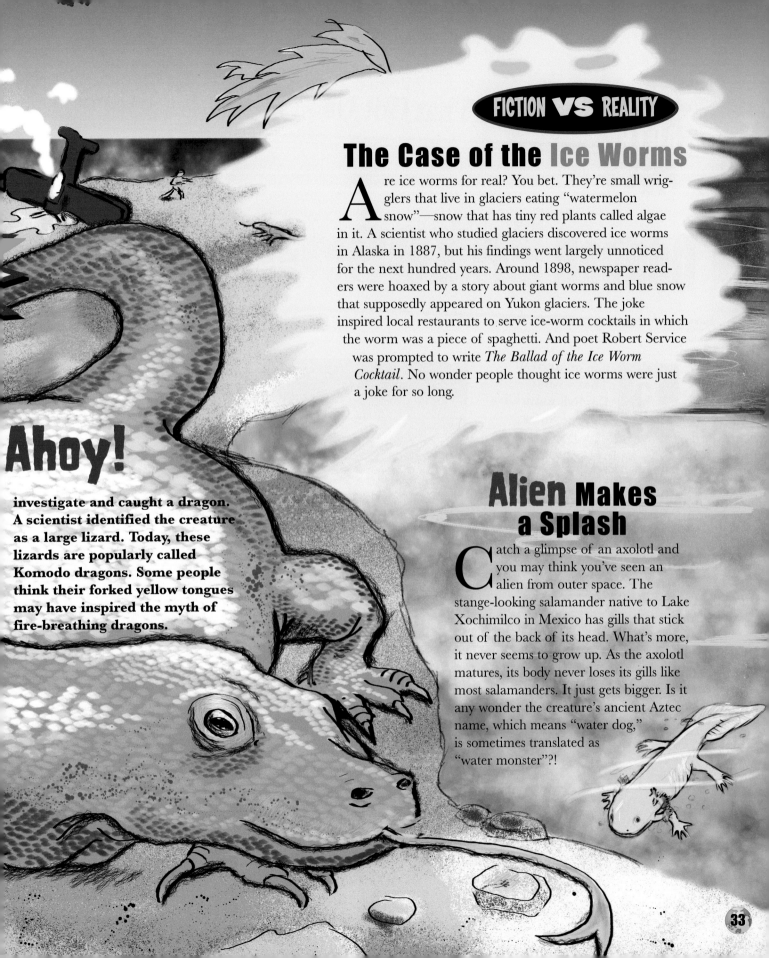

# The Case of the Ice Worms

Are ice worms for real? You bet. They're small wrigglers that live in glaciers eating "watermelon snow"—snow that has tiny red plants called algae in it. A scientist who studied glaciers discovered ice worms in Alaska in 1887, but his findings went largely unnoticed for the next hundred years. Around 1898, newspaper readers were hoaxed by a story about giant worms and blue snow that supposedly appeared on Yukon glaciers. The joke inspired local restaurants to serve ice-worm cocktails in which the worm was a piece of spaghetti. And poet Robert Service was prompted to write *The Ballad of the Ice Worm Cocktail*. No wonder people thought ice worms were just a joke for so long.

# Ahoy!

investigate and caught a dragon. A scientist identified the creature as a large lizard. Today, these lizards are popularly called Komodo dragons. Some people think their forked yellow tongues may have inspired the myth of fire-breathing dragons.

# Alien Makes a Splash

Catch a glimpse of an axolotl and you may think you've seen an alien from outer space. The stange-looking salamander native to Lake Xochimilco in Mexico has gills that stick out of the back of its head. What's more, it never seems to grow up. As the axolotl matures, its body never loses its gills like most salamanders. It just gets bigger. Is it any wonder the creature's ancient Aztec name, which means "water dog," is sometimes translated as "water monster"?!

# Oddball Fakes-Out Experts

**F**ake on arrival! That's what English naturalist George Shaw thought the platypus was when he first received its skin from Australia in 1799. How could a molelike creature with thick fur have a large beak like a duck?

He thought some joker probably sewed the furry animal skin onto a duck beak. After all, the skin had arrived via ship, and sailors were known for stitching together parts from different animals to fool naturalists into

**Say it's not "sew!"**

thinking they had a "new" animal on their hands.

But when more of the same specimens showed up, and naturalists studied them further, it became clear that the creature was for real.

While Australians called it a "water-mole," naturalists called it platypus for its flat feet. But then they found out there was already a beetle that went by the same name. Even so, the name platypus stuck, and the critter became famous for being a hoax that turned out to be the real thing after all. You might say nature had the last laugh!

The duck-billed platypus has a "sixth sense." It uses its beak to detect electric currents given off by prey.

# CHAPTER 5

# Earthlings' Best Friends

**M**eet the world's first astronaut and gnarliest surfer, and you just might think Earth has gone to the dogs—and cats! Everybody knows canines and felines are Earthlings' best friends. Dogs and cats nuzzled their way into this warm spot in Earthlings' hearts thousands of years ago, when people began keeping them as pets. Nowadays, the four-footed furballs are the most popular pets on the planet—and beyond. Find out why in this *Planet Earth News* exclusive.

Let's give them a round of a-paws!

# Who's that Kitty Cat?

**P**et cats may be cute and cuddly but, as many a cat-owner knows, they're also fiercely independent. Check out some of nature's quirks that make cats such lovable pets on Earth.

## Furball Walks
### Away from Ten-Story Fall

**D**id the scruffy furball have nine lives? Not likely. But cats do have a way of landing on their feet. As a feline falls through the air, specialized parts in its inner ears that control balance send messages to its brain to turn or flip its head right-side up. Then the rest of its body follows its head. That way, the cat can bring itself into the perfect position to land feet-first. Studies show that cats fracture fewer bones from falls seven-stories or higher than lower heights. No joke! Once a cat is falling at a steady speed, it relaxes, spreading out its legs like a parachute. And relaxed limbs are less likely to break on impact than tense ones. So sometimes it pays to be a cool cat!

## EXPOSED!

Who says cats don't like getting wet? Toby, a marmalade cat, goes surfing all the time with his owner in Ormond Beach, Florida.

## Climbing Down Is for the Birds

Cats are natural-born climbers. They love to climb up trees, furniture, and just about anything else that's standing around. As their front paws reach up for a "paw hold," gripping a tree like hooks, cats' strong hind leg muscles swiftly propel them up to another "paw hold." But while climbing up is a breeze, climbing down is another story altogether. That's because cats' back legs can't support their weight for them to climb down headfirst. What's more, their front claws curve around the wrong way for going down. No wonder cats get stuck up in trees or come down butt-first one awkward step after another.

## CAT BORN Bald

Gawk and squawk! That's what many Earthlings do when they see a Sphynx cat for the first time. Unlike nearly all other pet cats on the planet, the Sphynx is bald—and not just on its head but over its entire body. What's more, the big-eared feline has no whiskers and its furless skin is full of wrinkles. But despite its bald looks, the Sphynx is not completely hairless. It may have short hairs on a ridge down its back and on its muzzle, ears, tip of tail, and feet. Fine down also covers its skin, which is warm to the touch. In fact, Earthlings often say petting a Sphynx is like stroking a "suede hot-water bottle!"

## FICTION VS REALITY

## Here, Cloney, Cloney!

It's the stuff of science fiction. Clone Fluffy so you'll have a walking and talking, er, meowing, replica—genetic copycat—of your beloved kitty once she passes away. Well, in 1996, clones jumped from fiction to reality as scientists cloned a sheep named Dolly from the body cells of an adult sheep. Since then scientists have cloned cats, mice, cows, goats, pigs, and even horses. But get this: studies reveal that animals with exactly the same genes don't necessarily look and behave the same. So you can't expect a clone to be just like ol' Fluffy. Sometimes reality is stranger than fiction!

# Who Let the Dogs Out?

It's no secret dogs have a knack of nosing their way into the middle of things. Check out some of the things that make them Earthlings' best friends.

## TOY POODLE
### Plays Piano

Earthlings gasp in awe as Chanda-Leah tinkles her canine paws over the piano. Then when the fluffy poodle jumps on a skateboard, bowls like a pro, and fetches tissues for people who sneeze, audiences are completely bow-wowed. Chanda struts her stuff for young and old in schools, hospitals, and nursing homes. This doggy's bag of tricks includes spelling, adding, subtracting, and even multiplying.

In fact, the tail-wagging trickster holds the Guinness World Record for the most tricks performed by a dog. According to her owner, Sharon Robinson of Ontario, Canada, Chanda has more than 1,000 tricks up her paw. But Robinson's no professional trainer. She says Chanda's talents come from the poodle's natural behavior and intelligence. Now that's something to bark home about!

## Fido Sniffs Out the Stash

Fido and his canine pals are a nosy lot. They head everywhere they go nose-first and stop to sniff oodles of stuff along the way—including plain, old pavement. The fact is, sniffing around gives them a whiff of what's going down in the 'hood. Dogs' sense of smell is their most highly developed sense. They can smell odors that exist at concentrations about 100 million times lower than people can. Canines can also tell one scent from another and remember them. In fact, doggie brains store scent information just like a computer. No wonder some dogs use their schnozzle on the job to help people sniff out the stash—criminals hiding at the scene of a crime, flammable chemicals in burnt-down buildings, illegal drugs, bombs, explosives, and missing kids. Good dog!

# Pooch Is World's First Astronaut

On November 3, 1957, Laika, a stray mutt from the streets of Moscow, Russia, boldly went where no living creature had gone before. She blasted into orbit around Earth aboard the Russian satellite *Sputnik II*. American newspapers nicknamed her Muttnik, and news of the dog-onaut's mission shocked the world. In fact, many people were outraged, because Laika was hurtling toward certain death. Even though *Sputnik II* was equipped with life-support systems, air-conditioning, and jelly dogfood that Laika had been trained to eat, there was no way to recover it. Nevertheless, Russian scientists believed that creatures from Earth could survive in the weightlessness of space and went ahead with the mission to prove it. The trusty dog-onaut lived for a few hours until fright and over-heating got the best of her. And in so doing, the little mutt led the way for humans to rocket into space. You might say she let Earthlings off gravity's leash!

## Hoax Buster!

## DOG PRETENDS TO BE A CAT

Basenji dogs have no bark, no doggie odor, and clean themselves all over for hours on end, just like cats. In fact, one basenji owner describes his pet pooch as a "cat trapped in a dog's body." What do you think?

**Is the basenji...**

A) the real McCoy, er, dog breed?
B) a can of canine baloney?
C) a cat that looks like a dog?
D) a peculiar-acting pooch?

Answer on page 63.

## EXPOSED!

The old saying that dogs look like their owners just may be true. In a recent study, strangers correctly matched up owners and purebreds about two-thirds of the time by looking for similarities between the owners and the dogs!

# Monster Cat
## Surfs the Net

**L**et this cat out of the bag and you might have a monster on your hands. It's as big as a fat yellow lab, and it has a whopper of a tail, er, tale! A photo of the aptly named cat Snowball began prowling over the Internet in 2000.

According to a story that later accompanied the photo, Rodger Degagne claimed to have found two strays near a nuclear reactor. The strays had kittens, and Degagne gave the whole litter away except Snowball. Over time, Snowball's size, well, snow-

**A whale, er, tale of a cat.**

balled to a mondo 39 kg (87 lbs.).

The story explained that Snowball's parents may have been exposed to radiation at the reactor and passed it onto Snowball, resulting in the kitty's abnormal size. It sounded far-fetched, but the photo looked so real that people believed it.

However, once the photo appeared on a popular TV show Snowball's story melted on the spot. Cordell Hauglie of Washington, D.C. confessed that Snowball was his daughter's cat, Jumper, who weighed 9.5 kg (21 lbs.)—pretty heavy for a cat, but not monstrous. As a joke, he had altered a digital photo to create a huge kitty. Who knew the fake cat would live up to its name so well!

Leo, a cat of the Maine Coon breed, is the world's longest pet cat, measuring 121.9 cm (48 in.). In human height, Leo would stand 2.5 m (8 ft.) tall!

# CHAPTER 6

# Planet of the Bugs

**B**ug off! That's what you might be tempted to say if you were an alien invading Earth. After all, it's a planet where bugs rule. There are three times as many species on Earth that come from the ranks of insects than those of all other animals put together. You would encounter millions and millions of different insects on the march in the jungle, desert, and every other environment you ventured into.

Scientists think that insects are the most successful living organism to ever buzz around the planet. But that doesn't mean bugs are without enemies. Spiders have been one of their archenemy predators for millions of years. Scout out some crafty spiders and some extraordinary insects who know how to roll, er, crawl with the punches in this exclusive *Planet Earth News* field report.

The creepy crawlies are coming!

# Bugged for Survival?

Ever wonder if nature put a bug in insects' ears about survival? The fact is, insects do whatever it takes to stay alive. Check out some of their buggy survival moves.

## Twig Walks
### Off Tree

It looked like a twig, hung on a branch like a twig, and was perfectly still like a twig. Then it got up and walked right off the tree. Is it any wonder this long, skinny insect found throughout North America and the tropics is called a walkingstick? The twiglike appearance of the insect's exoskeleton, or outer shell, is a masterful disguise that conceals it from hungry predators. Nevertheless, once it starts to walk, it drops its disguise—but not its dupe-the-predator routine, or "schtick." The walkingstick may fall on the ground and play dead. Or it may even drop a leg to distract predators long enough to get away (a new leg grows a few weeks later). How's that for "schticking" it to your enemies?

## Headless Cockroach Lives!

If mastering survival were like mastering karate, the cockroach would be a blackbelt. The pesky master of survival began crawling over the planet long before the dinosaurs came and went. And its descendants are still going strong all over the globe. If it's too cold outside, the freeloading pest just moves in with people! It's a tough little menace to get rid of. Without its head, a roach can survive for a week. Without food, it can live for a month. What's more, as people develop poisons to kill it, the roach builds up resistance to withstand the chemicals. It also learns to keep out of areas where poisons often lay in wait. Now that's mind over matter—a bona fide blackbelt!

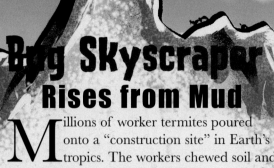

# Bug Skyscraper
## Rises from Mud

Millions of worker termites poured onto a "construction site" in Earth's tropics. The workers chewed soil and mixed it with spit, or saliva, to make a cementlike paste. Then, they molded the paste into walls that rose up and up. Once they were done, a virtual skyscraper stood 8 m (25 ft.) tall. The termites' tower boasted hundreds of apartments, natural air conditioning, and spires like a castle. Nevertheless, the termites built it for survival not luxury. Unlike many insects, termites have soft bodies that can quickly dry up in the sun. So they need a dark, damp place to live. No wonder they've become Earth's most skilled architects next to humans.

## Dancing for Dinner Is the New Buzz

When a honeybee finds a flower rich in nectar, it drinks up then returns to the hive and dances. If the flower is within 50 m (164 ft.), it dances in a circle. If the flower's farther away, it dances a figure-eight. Other bees follow the "dance directions" to pig out!

# Bugs Suck
## Sneaker Sweat

Not many people would consider a sweaty sneaker inviting, let alone refreshing. It's quite the contrary for butterflies. One time, a swarm of these insects began sucking on a sweaty sneaker drying in the sun! Butterflies survive on sugary nectar from flowers, but they also need salt and nitrogen. Human sweat contains both of these nutrients. So when the butterflies found the sweaty sneaker, it's quite likely they began sucking up the sweat. Yuck!

# Butterflies Spell
## the Alphabet

When it comes to spelling, butterflies wing it. The entire alphabet can be found on the wings of the world's butterflies! Over 30 years ago, photographer Kjell Sandved looked at a tropical butterfly through a microscope and noticed "a tiny perfect letter F hidden on the wing." Since then, he has trekked all over the world and found the rest of the letters of the alphabet written on butterfly wings.

# Beetlemania

**P**lanet Earth is in the throes of beetlemania. No joke! There are more kinds of beetles on the planet than plants or any other kind of animal. Check out some beetles in action.

## Bug Born to Scuba Dive

**T**he giant diving beetle is a natural-born scuba diver. This beetle, which preys on other insects and small fish, can stay underwater for hours without coming up for air. While a human scuba diver brings a tank of oxygen to breathe underwater, the giant diving beetle brings a bubble of air. It tucks the bubble under its hard front wings and uses long hairs that cover its hind legs like flippers. The air bubble absorbs oxygen from the water. So unlike an oxygen tank, it doesn't run out once the beetle uses up the original oxygen it contains. When the bubble becomes too small to give oxygen, the beetle surfaces to get another bubble—bloop!—and dives back down.

## Beetle Beats It

**W**hen the camphor beetle needs to make a quick get-away, it jetskis. No joke! The rice-grain-sized beetle hangs out on ponds, skating across the water on its legs. But if it senses predators near-by, look out. The beetle fires a gas out

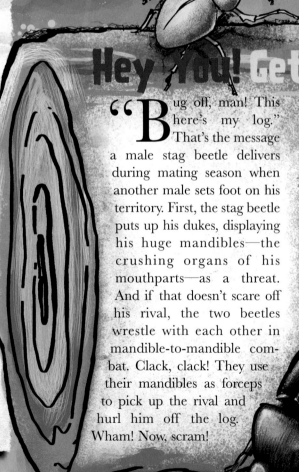

## Hey You! Get

"**B**ug off, man! This here's my log." That's the message a male stag beetle delivers during mating season when another male sets foot on his territory. First, the stag beetle puts up his dukes, displaying his huge mandibles—the crushing organs of his mouthparts—as a threat. And if that doesn't scare off his rival, the two beetles wrestle with each other in mandible-to-mandible combat. Clack, clack! They use their mandibles as forceps to pick up the rival and hurl him off the log. Wham! Now, scram!

## on Jetski

of its back legs that shoots it clear across the water! The tiny bug hurtles forward on its front feet, holding them out like skis, and steers by flexing its belly. How's that for blowing this pop, er, pond stand?

# Off of My Log!

## Beetle

### Has a Ball

*Roll, roll, roll your ball, gently like a wheel.*
*Speedily, speedily, speedily, speedily, life is but a meal.*

If a scarab beetle could sing, maybe that would be its anthem. The beetle flies upwind of elephants in the tropics. Once its antennae catch scent of any droppings, it lands on the poop and cuts it up to form a dung ball. The beetle sits on top of the ball, shaping it with its legs, making the ball bigger and bigger. Then it holds the ball with its hind legs and slides down headfirst until its front legs touch the ground. Next, it walks backwards, rolling the dung ball to its burrow to eat it. Mmm!

# Hoax Busters

## BIRD DROPPING
### WALKS OFF IN A HUFF

According to eyewitnesses in Brazil, a bird dropping picked itself up and walked away from the scene of the "splat" in broad daylight. What do you think?

**Did the eyewitnesses...**

A) see a beetle on the move?
B) make up their report as an April Fools' joke?
C) witness a quirk of nature?
D) lie like a rug?

Answer on page 63.

## EXPOSED!

One time, a 1.5 kg (3 lb.) fresh pile of elephant poop attracted 16,000 dung beetles. In just two hours, the beetles rolled away and gobbled up every scoop!

# Spiders

hey're creepy, they're crawly, and they're everywhere. Experts say that for every human on Earth, there are about 600,000 spiders. Check out how the eight-legged creatures get around.

## Hey Spidey
### Take a Hike, er, Kite!

ake off and go fly a kite! Maybe that's the message spider hatchlings get when competition for food within the brood becomes fierce. The fact is, many leave to fend for themselves by taking to the air like kites. No joke! Young spiders crawl onto the top of a rock or blade of grass. They turn to face the wind then tilt their abdomens up and spin out several strands of silk. The wind then draws up the silk strands along with the spider just like a kite on a string. While many spiders fly a couple of metres on the wind, some hang on for a long ride that carries them hundreds of kilometres. Now that's a kite that's truly out of sight!

## Love Bites—
### Arachnid Style

ill you be my valentine?" said the spider to the spider. Sound far-fetched? Well, male spiders often follow fancy courting rituals so the females don't mistake them for prey. Otherwise, the females, who are most often the larger of the two, may gobble them up. Gulp! When the male nursery-web spider goes courting, for example, he catches a fly, wraps it in silk, and gives it to the female as a gift. And if he can't find a fly, he wraps up a pebble instead. That way the female becomes occupied opening the gift and eating the bug, so the male can mate with her safely. Nevertheless, the male usually drops dead a bit later anyway. Whoa—that bites!

## Spider Puts On a **Happy Face**

The Hawaiian happy face spider keeps smiling no matter what. The little yellow spider that hangs out on the bottom of leaves in wet rain forests has the natural markings of a smiling face on its belly. In fact, its belly looks just like the happy face printed on T-shirts and stickers. But the smiley face on each spider is unique. Some have big eyes, some have red mouths, and some have eyebrows. Scientists think the happy faces may protect the spiders from being eaten by birds.

## Fly Drops in Uninvited

It sounds crazy. A fly heads for the center of a Mexican spider's web. But the center of the web isn't sticky. The fly can hang out there and pluck the web to lure the spider away from her eggs. Then the fly lays its larvae on the eggs and the larvae have a snack.

## Spider Lurks Under **Hidden Trapdoor**

The trapdoor spiders that live in hot spots around the world have a sneaky way of catching prey. They dig burrows in the ground, line the burrows with silk, and build snug-fitting trapdoors out of silk and soil at the top. The spiders attach a silk hinge to the trapdoor, so the door will swing open and shut. Then they cover up the trapdoor with plants and leaves, so unsuspecting prey can't see it. When nightfall comes, the spiders open the trapdoor halfway and stick out their front legs to lie in wait. Once tiny hairs on their legs pick up the vibrations of prey passing by, the spiders spring out, snatch the prey, and drag it into the burrow. Then the trapdoor slams shut and the spiders devour the prey in the comfort and safety of their own homes. In fact, some females never leave their burrows. Could it be they've fallen into a trap of their own design?

presents **Tales That Got Us**

# No Way Bumblebees Can Fly

**Mayday! Mayday!**

**P**ssst. Ever heard that bumblebees are freaks of nature? If not, you will. Sooner or later, someone, somewhere will tell you that bumblebees should not be able to fly. In the 1930s, someone will say, a flight scientist did a few calculations according to the laws of physics that govern Earth. And he showed that it's physically impossible for bumblebees to get off the ground!

Well, don't believe all the buzz you hear. The part of the tale that many people don't know is that the scientist made a mistake. He assumed that bumblebee wings are like flat plates, which are unsuited for flying. But when he looked at the wings under a microscope, he saw that they were shaped just like airplane wings.

Unfortunately, he found his error too late. The tale of his whiz-bang calculations was already aflutter around the world on its own wings. And to this day, it's never been grounded.

Bumblebees wing it with a loud buzz. Maybe that's because they have few predators to be wary of apart from skunks, who find them bee-licious—stinger and all.

# CHAPTER 7

# From the Ground Up

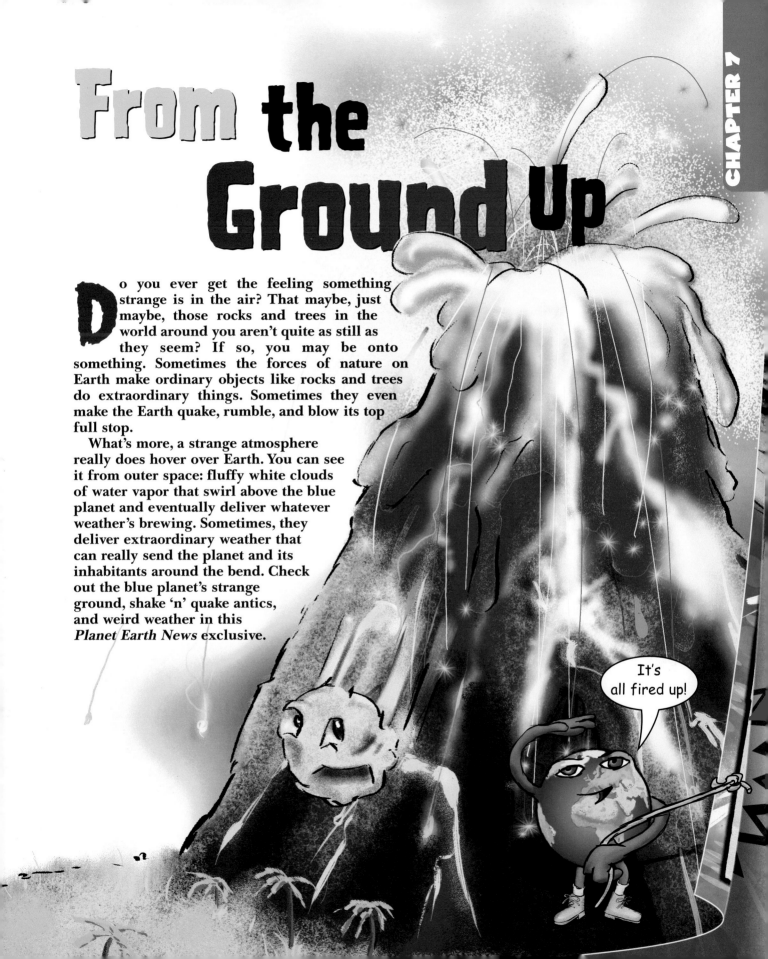

Do you ever get the feeling something strange is in the air? That maybe, just maybe, those rocks and trees in the world around you aren't quite as still as they seem? If so, you may be onto something. Sometimes the forces of nature on Earth make ordinary objects like rocks and trees do extraordinary things. Sometimes they even make the Earth quake, rumble, and blow its top full stop.

What's more, a strange atmosphere really does hover over Earth. You can see it from outer space: fluffy white clouds of water vapor that swirl above the blue planet and eventually deliver whatever weather's brewing. Sometimes, they deliver extraordinary weather that can really send the planet and its inhabitants around the bend. Check out the blue planet's strange ground, shake 'n' quake antics, and weird weather in this *Planet Earth News* exclusive.

It's all fired up!

# Strange Ground

**H**ey Earthling! Chances are you rarely give the ground beneath your feet a second thought. But if you were to look closely and prick up your ears, you'd discover some bizarre stuff underfoot.

## Trees Turn

**N**o, the logs lying on the ground in Arizona's Petrified Forest haven't been scared stiff. Nevertheless, they've turned to solid stone. Millions of years ago, when dinosaurs ruled the Earth, the petrified logs were giant trees. The tree trunks stretched as much as 2.7 m (9 ft.) wide and shot up almost 61 m (200 ft.) into the sky. When wind or floodwater knocked down the towering trees into rivers and streams, the trees

## These Rocks are Made for Walkin'

**S**trange things go on in Death Valley, California. Take the case of the mysterious moving rocks. No one's ever seen them move, and they don't move often. But when they do, they leave trails in the valley's dry lake bed. What's going on? Some scientists think the rocks walk only when certain conditions take hold of them. First, a thin layer of ice freezes over the lake bed. This ice sheet lifts the rocks up ever so slightly and freezes the rocks within it. Then wind blows the ice sheet around the lake bed, dragging the rocks along for the ride! But not all scientists agree with this explanation—and the rocks aren't talking. So the mystery of the walking rocks is still, as they say, footloose and fancy-free.

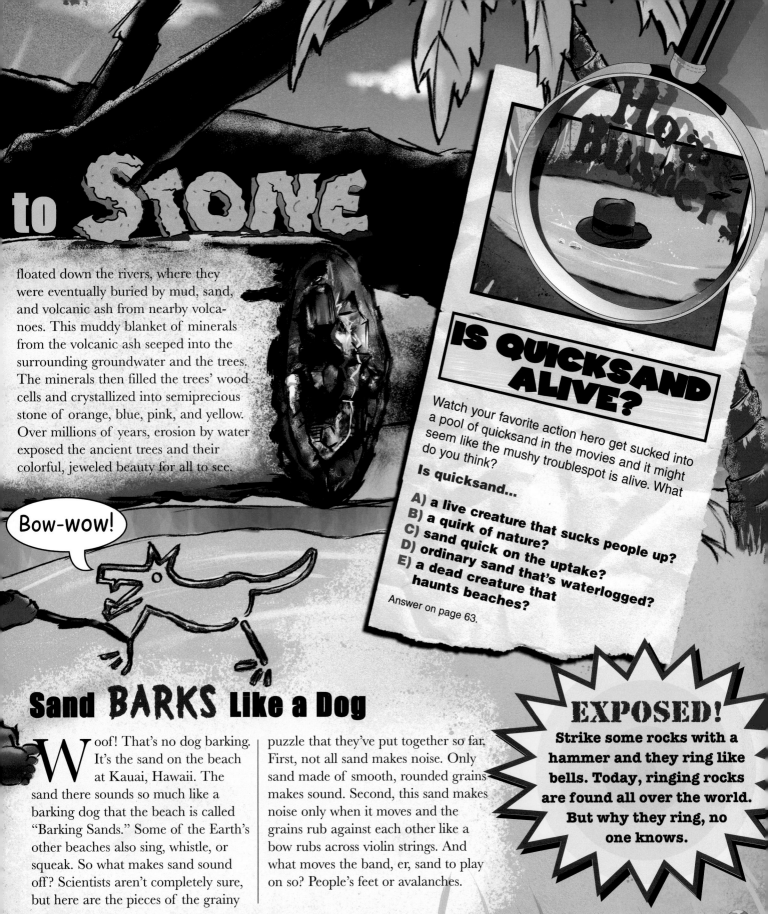

# to STONE

floated down the rivers, where they were eventually buried by mud, sand, and volcanic ash from nearby volcanoes. This muddy blanket of minerals from the volcanic ash seeped into the surrounding groundwater and the trees. The minerals then filled the trees' wood cells and crystallized into semiprecious stone of orange, blue, pink, and yellow. Over millions of years, erosion by water exposed the ancient trees and their colorful, jeweled beauty for all to see.

Bow-wow!

## IS QUICKSAND ALIVE?

Watch your favorite action hero get sucked into a pool of quicksand in the movies and it might seem like the mushy troublespot is alive. What do you think?

Is quicksand...

A) a live creature that sucks people up?
B) a quirk of nature?
C) sand quick on the uptake?
D) ordinary sand that's waterlogged?
E) a dead creature that haunts beaches?

Answer on page 63.

## Sand BARKS Like a Dog

Woof! That's no dog barking. It's the sand on the beach at Kauai, Hawaii. The sand there sounds so much like a barking dog that the beach is called "Barking Sands." Some of the Earth's other beaches also sing, whistle, or squeak. So what makes sand sound off? Scientists aren't completely sure, but here are the pieces of the grainy puzzle that they've put together so far. First, not all sand makes noise. Only sand made of smooth, rounded grains makes sound. Second, this sand makes noise only when it moves and the grains rub against each other like a bow rubs across violin strings. And what moves the band, er, sand to play on so? People's feet or avalanches.

## EXPOSED!

Strike some rocks with a hammer and they ring like bells. Today, ringing rocks are found all over the world. But why they ring, no one knows.

# Shake 'n' Quake Planet

**D**oes Earth really rock your world? You bet! For starters, Earth is never still underground, and sometimes it really blows its top. Check out how it gushes, quakes, and belches molten rock!

## Earth Quakes in Its Boots

**E**arth quakes about a million times a year. Luckily, most of those earthquakes are too faint to notice. Phew! But every once in a while, Earth really quakes in its boots when parts of its crust, or outer shell, suddenly move. These shifts often occur along cracks, or faults, where two parts of the crust crunch together, push apart, or slide past each other. The sudden movement shakes all the surrounding rock, sending out shockwaves. Then, depending on how close you are to the quake's source, the ground beneath your feet may tremble. Windows may rattle, parked cars may sway back and forth, and buildings may topple over.

## Earth Blows off Steam

**O**n May 2, 2000, Steamboat, the world's tallest active geyser, went off for the first time in nine years. The gushing hot spring in Yellowstone National Park erupted with a major blast. The unpredictable old geyser shook the ground, roared, and fired a tall stream of boiling water into the air. And once it stopped gushing, the old geyser blew off a thunderous jet of steam about 152 m (500 ft.) tall. Geysers pop up in spots where active or recently active volcanoes lie, such as Wyoming, Iceland, and New Zealand. Molten rock in these areas superheats ground-water, turning it into steam that builds into enormous pressure. Eventually, this steam and hot water get forced out of the ground and the geysers blow. What a rush, er, gush!

## One-Eyed Planet

It looks like an eye! That's what you might think if you saw Grand Prismatic Spring from above. This hot spring supports heat-loving bacteria that may hold clues to how life first formed on Earth. Talk about having an eye on the world!

## Earth: Uh-oh! I'm Gonna Hurl!

Kilauea just can't help it. The Earth's most active volcano sits atop the Big Island of Hawaii, spewing up lava day after day. In fact, the name Kilauea means "spewing" in Hawaiian. The volcano oozes enough lava to fill 45,000 dump trucks daily, and shows no sign of putting a cork in the flow. Kilauea sits on an area of Earth's crust where hot liquid rock, or magma, blasts through from deep within the Earth. The volcano expels a river of red-hot lava that can bury, melt, or set fire to anything in its path. The lava flows into the sea, turning water into steam and sparking explosions that hurl water, rocks, and molten lava into the air. The lava then cools to form new rocks. What a relief!

## EXPOSED!

What rumbles, smells like rotten eggs, and flings mud? A mud volcano! Mud volcanoes are small cone-shaped mounds of mud and clay that Earth heaves up from below.

## Ocean Cooks Up an Island

In November 1963, people all over the world had their eyes glued on the ocean off the coast of Iceland. The sea was on fire! Clouds of steam rose, rocks exploded out of the water, and black smoke climbed high into the sky. The fiery spectacle was the birth of an island as hot magma shot up from a volcano erupting on the sea floor. Over several months, the island took shape from steady lava flows. Today, it is a living laboratory for scientists studying how plants and animals come ashore and move in.

# It Fell From the Sky

As any Earthling will say, the weather on Earth—rain, snow, hail, tornadoes, lightning—is often unpredictable and sometimes totally wacky. Check out some truly riveting, er, ribbiting rain that fell from the sky.

## EXPOSED!

In August 2003, rain fell in the Annapolis Valley, Canada, every day for 13 days straight. Farmers' fields got so soggy that beans rusted and heads of lettuce swelled up and exploded.

## It's Raining Frogs
### And Frogs

Plop! Plop! Ribbit! Ribbit! What a strange sound that is, thought the people of Naphilion, Greece, one morning in 1981. To their surprise, it was the sound of small green frogs falling from the sky, landing in trees, yards, and streets.

And what really got the townspeople hopping was that the frogs were native to North Africa! How had the little croakers become airborne to travel hundreds of kilometres away from their home? Some scientists suspect that waterspouts—tornadolike funnels of swirling air that form over water—may suck up creatures near the surface and carry them aloft. Then, wherever the waterspouts die out, they dump the critters back to Earth.

# SKY TO EARTH:
# BOMBS AWAY

Look out below! Frogs aren't the only creatures to fall from the sky. Far from it. Check out other kinds of wacky rain that have bombarded Earth.

## Strange BUT True

### Truly Twisted

Tornadoes, or spinning windstorms, can whip up winds that reach 500 km (310 mi.) per hour and rip apart almost anything they meet. One tornado scooped up a chicken in a cage, plucked all the bird's feathers, then set the cage down!

**Gator Rain**
**Crash Site:** In 1877, several alligators rained down on a farm in South Carolina, and crawled around unharmed.

**Shellshocking Rain**
**Crash Site:** In 1881, a thunderstorm dumped tons of hermit crabs and periwinkle snails in Worcester, England.

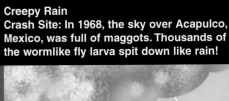

**Creepy Rain**
**Crash Site:** In 1968, the sky over Acapulco, Mexico, was full of maggots. Thousands of the wormlike fly larva spit down like rain!

**Fishy Rain**
**Crash Site:** In 1989, rainstorms showered houses in Ipswich, Australia, with hundreds of sardines.

**Slimy Rain**
**Crash Site:** In 1996, fierce thunderstorms slimed houses in Southern Tasmania by dropping either fish eggs or jellyfish.

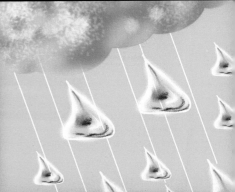

**Monster Rain**
**Crash Site:** In 2004, scientists in Brazil saw 1-cm (3/8-in.) wide raindrops—the biggest ever recorded on Earth.

# Attack of the Giant Ice Balls

**W**hoosh! A ball of ice as big as a basketball plummeted toward Earth in January 2000. The 2-kg (4-lb.) ice ball crashed onto the windshield of a parked car in Spain. Then it broke in two and fell to the ground. Kerplunk! Over the next week, several more basketball-sized chunks of ice fell from Spanish skies. Bing! Bang! Boom!

Nobody was more baffled about the source of the ice balls than the scientists called in to investigate.

**An alien slam dunk?**

One theory said the balls were supersized hailstones. But it didn't fly because hail forms during thunderstorms and there wasn't a cloud in the sky when the giant ice balls fell. Another theory said the balls were frozen waste flushed from jet planes passing overhead. Still another said the ice balls were chunks of comet dust that fell to Earth. Nothing seemed to fit.

So the mystery of the giant ice balls continues until scientists crack the case— or a hoaxster owns up to an incredible prank of deception!

**Sometimes thunderclouds are like giant pea-shooters. They develop and release hailstones the size of peas.**

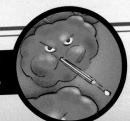

# CHAPTER 8

# The Outer Limits

Earth hangs out with the stars night and day. But it's no planet Hollywood or celebrity wannabe. Its local galaxy of stars is the Milky Way—a system of 100 billion stars.

Earth's neighborhood star is the Sun. The blue planet orbits the Sun along with nine other neighboring planets. And as everybody knows, Earthlings are curious about their neighbors, especially the Moon and Mars, which they've peeked at with binoculars, telescopes, and fly-by cameras!

And when the view wasn't clear enough to see what was going on in their neighbors' backyards, Earthlings' imaginations seemed to know no limits. Visions of green cheese and ancient aliens popped into their heads. Get the inside story on the outer limits according to Earthlings in this *Planet Earth News* exclusive.

Blast off!

# The Moon

**N**o other planet in our galactic neighborhood has a Moon quite like Earth's. Check out what the ol' craterface is made of and some of the loony tunes it plays upon our planet.

## No Hunk of
## Green Cheese

**O**K, maybe we didn't need astronauts to tell us the Moon is not made of green cheese. But until the *Apollo* astronauts set foot on it in 1969, no one knew what the Moon was made of. No one knew if any water or living things ran around its surface. No one even knew if the astronauts' feet would meet firm ground or sink into dust several centimetres deep! As it turned out, the astronauts stepped onto a powdery surface made of basalt rock. They discovered that the Moon is drier than any desert on Earth. They found no soil, no water, nor any sign of life. Over several missions, astronauts brought back 381 kg (841 lbs.) of Moon rocks. Heavy stuff!

## Big Whack
### Throws Moon for a Loop

**W**hiz! Bang! Boom! Billions of years ago, in a galaxy we now call home, meteorites and chunks of rock as big as small planets were whizzing through space helter skelter, crashing headlong into Earth and other planets that hung out around the Sun—a.k.a our solar system. These spectacular collisions melted the planets' rock, hollowed out craters, and built up the planets' bulk. In fact, no living thing could have survived them. Back then, Earth had no life and no Moon to hang with. But it did have a next-door neighbor, Theia, a planet the size of Mars. The two planets hung out together for millions

# Earth Grooves
## to Loony Tunes

Life on Earth as we know it might not exist without the Moon. For starters, the Big Whack that formed the white orb (see below) wiped out any early thick atmosphere of gases that may have made Earth's surface unsuitable for the first life-forms that rose up and evolved into the creatures that thrive all over the planet today. Second up, the giant impact left Earth tilted on its axis. And this tilt creates seasons by exposing different parts of the planet to different amounts of sunlight during the year as Earth orbits the Sun. What's more, the Moon's gravity, or force which attracts Earth, helps keep Earth stable. Without it, Earth might wobble up and down like Mars, plunging areas into varying bouts of darkness. And as the Moon's gravity pulls on the oceans, it creates high and low tides, which many living things follow in their daily quest for food (see Crab has Wicked Spitball, page 28). Who knew the Moon's loony tunes were so groovy?!

of years. Eventually, the onslaught of meteorites and rocks died down. But all was not calm. Something had put Earth and Theia on a collision course and there was no stopping them. Theia hurtled closer and closer to Earth and then—whack!—slammed into the world with the energy of trillions of bombs. Ka-BOOM! The collision hurled chunks of Earth and Theia into the sky. Over time, the chunks clumped together to form the Moon and loop around, or orbit, Earth. And that, according to scientists, is the Big Whack theory of how the Moon became a chip off the old rock and then some!

## FICTION VS REALITY
## Did We Really Land on the Moon?

Can you imagine a world in which Earthlings had never gone to the Moon or outer space? In 2000, William Hartmann published a science-fiction story in which David, a boy living in 2063, is brainwashed into believing space exploration never happened. And just one year after it was published, the story seemed to get real when a TV documentary aired, claiming we never really went to the Moon. Suddenly, kids and teachers everywhere began emailing NASA (the National Aeronautics and Space Administration which carried out the *Apollo* Moon missions). "Hey, dude," they wrote, "did we go or didn't we?" NASA came back with, "Yes—no ifs, buts, or doubts about it." And they pointed to the 381 kg (841 lbs.) of Moon rocks that the astronauts lugged back as proof positive. First off, the rocks are unlike any rocks found on Earth. Secondly, 142 independent scientists around the world have examined them. And thirdly, scientists say they're impossible to fake.

## EXPOSED!

The Moon's got "pull." When it's directly over North America, the Moon's force of gravity can pull the whole landmass up as much as 15 cm (1/2 ft.)!

# Mars, the Red Planet

**M**ars is the most Earthlike planet in our solar system. So when Earthlings began wondering if anybody else is out there, it seemed like a good place to look. Check out what we've discovered about the red planet and how some "discoveries" depend on our point of view.

## Fly-By Missions Kill Off Martians

**B**y the 1960s, many Earthlings—not just scientists—wondered whether life existed on Mars. Popular images of Martians included little green men with big brain sacs for heads and long arm tentacles. But in 1964, the space probe *Mariner 4* flew by Mars and sent back photos that killed off these notions of Martians. The photos showed no trace of any canals and revealed that the surface of Mars was dotted with craters like those on the Moon. In 1976, scientists sent another space probe to test Martian soil for the building blocks of life. It found not a one! Mars is a dead world, concluded many scientists with a sigh.

## Canals on Mars
### Built by Martians

**E**xtraordinary! Maybe that's what astron-omers Giovanni Schiaparelli and Percival Lowell thought when they looked at Mars through their telescopes in the late 1800s. Working 17 years apart, both men recorded and mapped the maze of black lines, or channels, that they saw criss-crossing the surface of Mars.

Back then, telescopic views of Mars were fuzzy and unclear. So it was common for different people to see different things. Lowell said the dark lines were canals built by Martians to carry water to dry deserts. Such ideas electrified the public and inspired many science-fiction novels and films over the next 50 years.

## EXPOSED!

In 2004, opportunity knocked. The rover *Opportunity* crawled across Mars with a microscope and rock drill and discovered that the red planet was once drenched with water—the all-important ingredient of life.

## Hoax Buster

## FACE LAUNCHES A THOUSAND BELIEVERS

On July 25, 1976, the *Viking 1* spacecraft orbiting Mars snapped a photo, revealing a human face 1 km (1 mi.) wide on the surface of the red planet. NASA scientists said the face was a huge rock with shadows falling upon it that formed the illusion of eyes, nose, and a mouth. But some scientists thought it was an alien monument like the ancient Egyptian pyramids, proving that intelligent beings lived on Mars. And this idea fired up many a believer around the world. What do you think?

**Is the face on Mars...**

A) a hoax?
B) a Martian monument?
C) a thought-provoking photo?
D) a rock with shadows on it?

Answer on page 63.

# Martians Rise from the Dead

Thanks to extremophiles, the search for life on Mars isn't dead yet. No, they're not "extreme believers." Extremophiles are creatures that live in extreme environments on Earth, such as bacterialike organisms that thrive near deep sea vents heated by volcanoes. Since their recent discovery, extremophiles have changed our view of life. They don't depend on the organic building blocks most life does. What's more, scientists think they may have been the first life-form on Earth, and that early Mars may have been an even better place for them. So there's a chance that extremophiles, or organisms like them, may be alive and well underneath the surface of the red planet. And sooner or later, Earthlings may just have to find out....

presents **Tales That Got Us**

# Martians Invade with Death Rays

'T was the night before Halloween 1938, when all through America not a creature was sleeping, not even a kid.

The people were glued to their radios with shock in hopes that a miracle soon would be there.

Back then, there was no TV to watch or Internet, so people listened to the radio to get their kicks and the news. And that night the Mercury Theatre radio program had decided to give listeners an extra-special

**Trick or treat?**

Halloween treat—a radio play version of H.G. Wells's popular sci-fi novel *The War of the Worlds*, in which Martians invade Earth.

The only problem was that thousands of listeners thought the Martian invasion was for real! And as the play's realistic "news bulletins" hit the airwaves, announcing that octopuslike Martians armed with death rays had landed in New Jersey, they believed them. Some people were so scared they packed up their kids, cars, and all and drove for the hills.

H.G. Wells is often called the father of science fiction. He wrote the novel *The First Men in the Moon* in 1901—and 68 years later, Earthlings actually did land on the Moon.

# Answers

### Tide Makes River Run Backwards, page 11

Give yourself five points if you chose C, or ten points if you chose D. The Bay of Fundy has the highest tides in the world. At low tide, the St. John River flows downstream toward the bay. At high tide, water flows into the bay and the further inland it flows, the higher the bay's narrowing sides force it to go. When the bay water reaches the same height as the river, the flow of the river stops completely. Eventually, the bay water rises higher than the river water and the force of this high tide begins to push the river water upstream.

### UFOs Make Crop Circles, page 17

If you chose E, give yourself five points or, if you picked A, ten points. In 1991, Doug Bower and Dave Chorley of Wiltshire County, England, confessed to making the circles that had appeared over 20 years. The pair of pranksters demonstrated how they used a wood plank suspended from a rope to push down ripe crops, making circles similar to those that had been found. Still, many people doubted the pair's claim to fame and didn't believe they could have made the hundreds of circles that had cropped up over the years—especially those formed outside England. Also, in 1993, the BMW car company secretly made a circle in a rye field in South Africa as a publicity stunt. The circle looked like their company logo. Nevertheless, in the minds of many, the origin of crop circles remains an unsolved mystery.

### Fairy Ring Appears Overnight, page 23

If you chose any answer but C, give yourself five points. You didn't fall for the legend that magical fairies make mushroom rings as they dance in circles in the night, which many people believed long ago. In fact, "fairy rings," the common name for mushroom rings, comes from this legend. If you chose B, give yourself ten points. Scientists say fungi naturally form fairy rings. The body, or mycelium, of some fungi grows underground, spreading outward in a circle. Eventually, individual mushrooms pop up around the outer edge of the mycelium. Fairy rings grow in open grass and forests. Some grow outward as much as 20 cm (8 in.) a year. One in France is 600 m (1/2 mi.) wide, and scientists think it's 700 years old!

### Fish Walks to New Digs, page 29

Give yourself five points if you chose C, or ten points if you chose D. The walking catfish of Africa, Asia, and Florida can wriggle across land on the tips of its fins by flexing its body. It walks from lake to lake when its watery home dries up and sometimes it goes for a stroll to look for food. As the fish prowls across land, it breathes air through an organ shaped like tree branches.

### Dog Pretends to be a Cat, page 39

Give yourself five points if you chose D, or ten points if you chose A. The basenji is a real dog whose origins lie in Africa. It has a wrinkly forehead, curly tail, and racehorse gait. It's often called the "barkless dog," because it doesn't bark. But that doesn't mean it's quiet. Far from it! Basenjis yodel, chortle, and growl. And believe it or not, the quirky canines really do have no doggie stink and groom themselves like cats.

### Bird Dropping Walks Off in a Huff, page 45

Give yourself five points if you chose C, and ten points if you chose A. When one type of Brazilian beetle gets alarmed it disguises itself as a bird dropping. It folds up its legs and shows its white underbelly. Then it stretches one white leg askew to give the "dropping" a splatter effect. (Who knew beetles were so adept at special effects?) So chances are the eyewitnesses saw this beetle scuttle off once it sensed the coast was clear of predators.

### Is Quicksand Alive? page 51

Give yourself five points if you chose B, and ten points if you chose D. Believe it or not, scientists say quicksand is just ordinary sand that has become extremely waterlogged. It can form anywhere. When sand mixes with lots of water, the water separates the sand grains. The result? The sand turns from "solid ground" to more of a mushy liquid, which can no longer support much weight. So if you step on it, you'll sink. And if you struggle or thrash around, you'll sink even faster. But if you relax, you'll float!

### Face Launches a Thousand Believers, page 61

Give yourself five points if you chose C, or ten points if you chose D. According to NASA scientists, the Face on Mars is just a rock with shadows on it. And although NASA never believed Martians had sculpted the face, the idea that they had spread like wildfire through the public. So NASA wanted to get a clearer photograph to prove the thing was a rock once and for all. In 1998, another Mars probe took a shot that was ten times sharper than the original photo. This photo showed the face was a rock. But some people were less than satisfied. They said that clouds in the photo covered part of the face. So in 2001, the Mars probe flew by for another shot. And this time it got a clear shot that showed cracks in the rock and no trace of any eyes, mouth, or nose. Still, some die-hard believers refused to face it. They said NASA had doctored the photo to cover up the existence of the Face!

### If your score is between:

- 80 and 60, you're a Shrewd Hoax Bustin' Dude. You know phony baloney when you see it. But you don't like to jump to any conclusions until you've considered all the facts and angles.

- 55 and 25, you're a Clever Hoax Buster. You like to size up the situation and examine the facts to draw your conclusions.

- 20 and 0, you're a Hoax Buster in Training. You jump to conclusions quickly. But if you slow down and give yourself time to go over all the facts and angles, you can become a Hoax-Busting ace.

*Hoax Busters How did you do?*

# Index